To Edward Stansfield (aka Ed) with bubbles – T.M.
For My – A.P.

KINGFISHER
An imprint of Kingfisher Publications Plc
New Penderel House, 283-288 High Holborn, London WC1V 7HZ
www.kingfisherpub.com

First published by Kingfisher 2006
2 4 6 8 10 9 7 5 3 1

Text copyright © Tony Mitton 2006
Illustrations copyright © Ant Parker 2006

ISBN-13: 978 0 7534 1269 5
ISBN-10: 0 7534 1269 1

Printed in Singapore
1TR/0506/TWP/SGCH(SGCH)/170ENSOMA/C

Super SUBMARINES

Tony Mitton
and
Ant Parker

KINGFISHER

A submarine's a kind of boat
that dives beneath the sea.

To travel down it takes in water
till its tanks are full -

Below the waves is such a strange
and wondrous place to be.

When it's underwater
the propeller makes it go.
The hydroplanes can tilt to steer it
up or down, like so.

the weight of water gives the submarine
a downward pull.

The rudder also steers the sub
and turns it left or right.
Computers help to navigate -
down deep there's not much light.

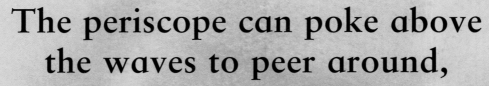

The periscope can poke above
the waves to peer around,

but further down, the submarine depends on sonar sound.

which bounces back to help them guess
what's out there in the deep.

A submarine needs crew
to keep it running night and day.

The crew need living quarters,
where they eat and rest and play.

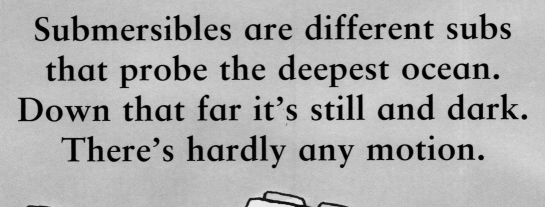

Submersibles are different subs
that probe the deepest ocean.
Down that far it's still and dark.
There's hardly any motion.

But even there submersibles
discover deep-sea creatures,
which glow or carry lanterns
and have very funny features.

Submersibles are used to rescue
divers, or explore.
They sometimes salvage sunken wrecks
upon the ocean floor.

They're used to service oil rigs,
lay cables and fix pipes.
Their robot subs have cameras
and arms of many types.

But look! Our sub is rising -
its work below is done.

Very soon the busy crew
will see the sky and sun.

Its ballast tanks have emptied - they've pushed the water out.

The submarine is back in dock.
"Hooray!" the sailors shout.

Submarine bits

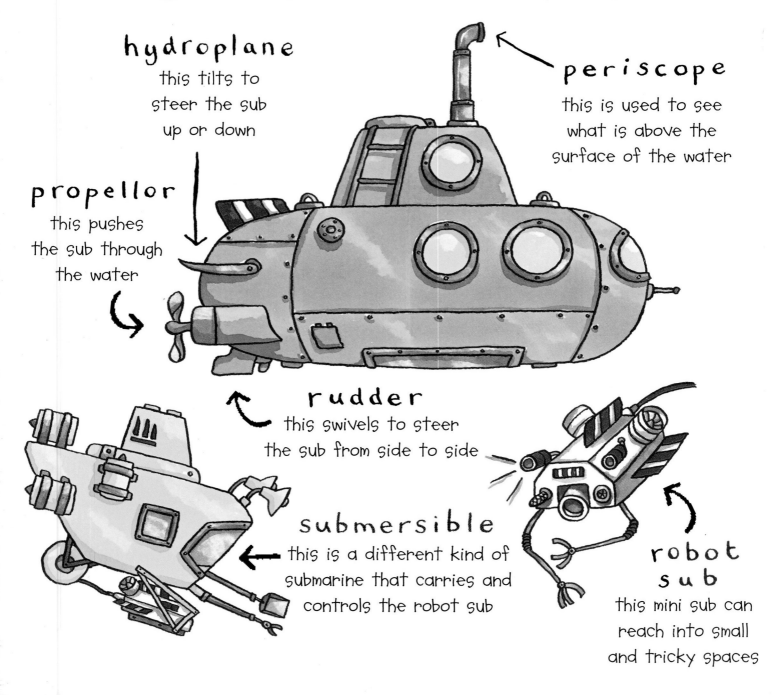

hydroplane
this tilts to steer the sub up or down

periscope
this is used to see what is above the surface of the water

propellor
this pushes the sub through the water

rudder
this swivels to steer the sub from side to side

submersible
this is a different kind of submarine that carries and controls the robot sub

robot sub
this mini sub can reach into small and tricky spaces